# Viola Time Jog...

## Viola accompaniment book

### Kathy and David Blackwell

---

**Teacher's note**

These duet parts are written to accompany the tunes in *Viola Time Joggers*. They are an alternative to the piano accompaniments or audio tracks, and are not designed to be used with those items. A separate violin duet book is available providing duet parts for when violas play together with violins using *Fiddle Time Joggers*.

Kathy and David Blackwell

---

## OXFORD
### UNIVERSITY PRESS

Great Clarendon Street, Oxford OX2 6DP, England
This collection © Oxford University Press 2005, 2013, and 2022
Unless marked otherwise, all pieces (music and words) are by Kathy and David Blackwell and are
© Oxford University Press. All traditional pieces are arranged by Kathy and David Blackwell and are
© Oxford University Press. Unauthorized arrangement or photocopying of this copyright material is ILLEGAL.

Kathy and David Blackwell have asserted their right under the Copyright,
Designs and Patents Act, 1988, to be identified as the Composers of this Work.

Impression: 2

ISBN: 978-0-19-356214-1

Music and text origination by Katie Johnston
Printed in Great Britain on acid-free paper by
Halstan & Co. Ltd, Amersham, Bucks.

# Contents

# 1. Bow down, O Belinda

American folk tune

pizz.

arco

mf

# 2. Under arrest!

KB & DB

pizz.

(arco)

f

Four short crot - chets
Four short quar - ter -

(⊓)

mp sim.

played on G, (rest) one fell off and left just three. (rest)
- notes on G,

1 2 3, (rest) 1 2 3, (rest) one fell off and left just three. (rest)

cresc. mf

Say the word 'rest' quietly to yourself as you play.

3

## 3. Someone plucks, someone bows

Traditional
Words KB & DB

Down, up goes the bow, when we're play - ing fast or slow;

Down, up goes the bow, when we're play - ing high or low.

## 4. Down up

C string special

KB & DB

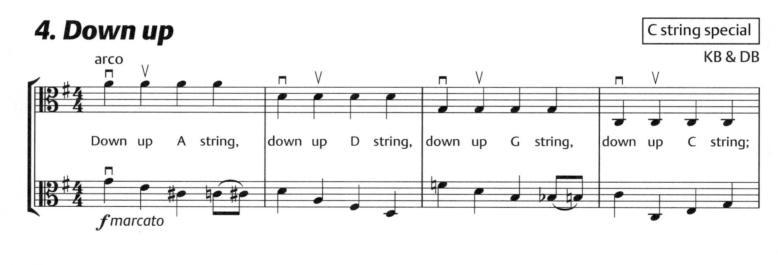

Down up A string, down up D string, down up G string, down up C string;

*f marcato*

\* Play the D and end with G.

\* Fill in the letter names of these notes.

# 5. Two in a boat

American folk tune

# 6. London Bridge

English folk tune

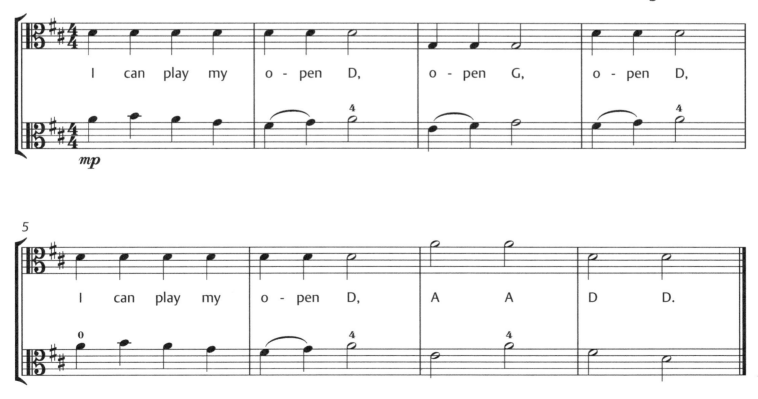

I can play my o - pen D, o - pen G, o - pen D,

I can play my o - pen D, A A D D.

# 7. Fast lane

KB & DB

Try even faster the second time through!

# 8. In flight

**Calmly**

KB & DB

*p* legato

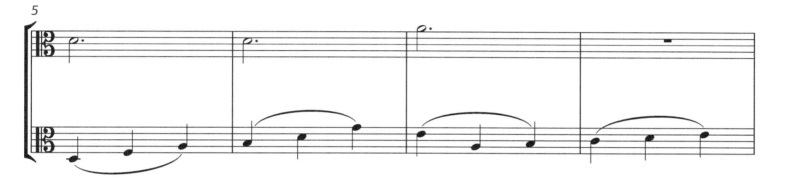

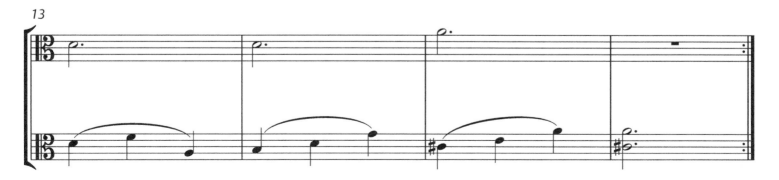

In the rests, let your bow make a circle as you swoop and soar like a bird.

# 9. Lift off!

KB & DB

Lift your bow off in each of the rests and let it orbit! (Make a circle with your right arm.)

# 10. Katie's waltz

KB & DB

## 11. Copy cat

KB & DB

# 12. Tap dancer

KB & DB

\* Hold the bow upright and tap the screw end of the bow on your music stand.

10

# 13. Rhythm fever

KB & DB

**Rock tempo**

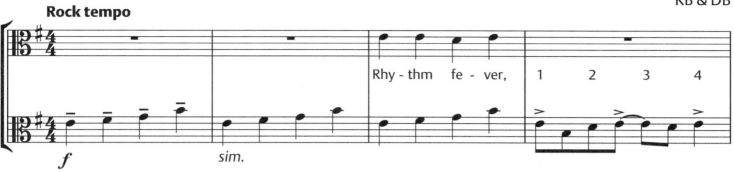

*f*         *sim.*

Rhy - thm fe - ver, 1 2 3 4

feel the beat, 1 2 3 4 feel the rhy - thm, 1 2 3 4

in your feet. 1 2 3 4 Feel the rhy - thm as you play it,

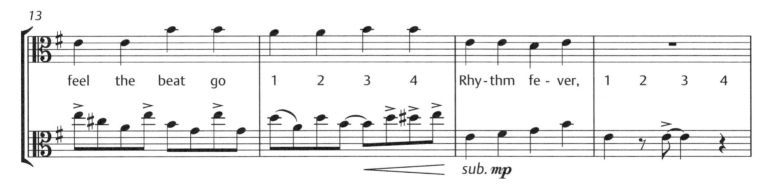

feel the beat go 1 2 3 4 Rhy - thm fe - ver, 1 2 3 4

*sub. **mp***

rhy - thm fe - ver, 1 2 3 4 rhy - thm fe - ver, oh yeah!

*mf*        *f*

## 14. Here it comes!

KB & DB

Through the teeth and past the gums, so watch out, tum - my, here it comes!

Through the teeth and past the gums, so watch out, tum - my, here it comes!

\* Think of a foody rhythm and play it on these notes.

## 15. So there!

KB & DB

**Brightly**

pizz. arco pizz. arco

cresc.

ff

So there!

# 16. Rowing boat

KB & DB

Gently

mp

Getting slower

p

## 17. Ally bally

Scottish folk tune

## 18. Tiptoe, boo!

KB & DB

**Spookily!**

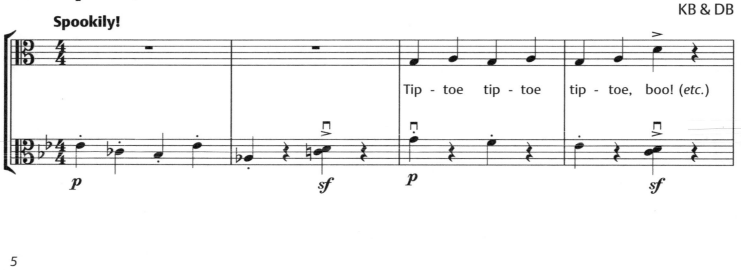

Tip - toe   tip - toe   tip - toe,  boo! (*etc.*)

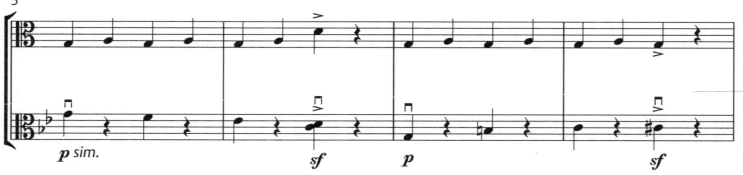

The pupil's part may also be played pizzicato.

## 19. Travellin' slow

KB & DB

## 20. C string boogie

C string special

KB & DB

* Turn around or, if you are sitting, stand up and sit down again!

# 21. Off to Paris

French folk tune

## 22. Clare's song

KB & DB

**Gently**

rit.

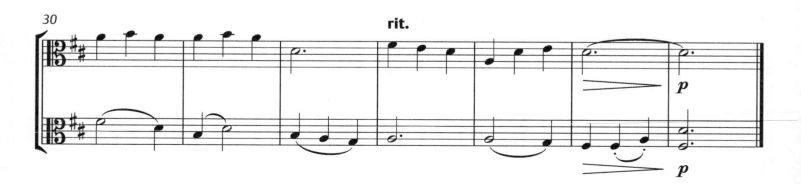

## 23. City lights

KB & DB

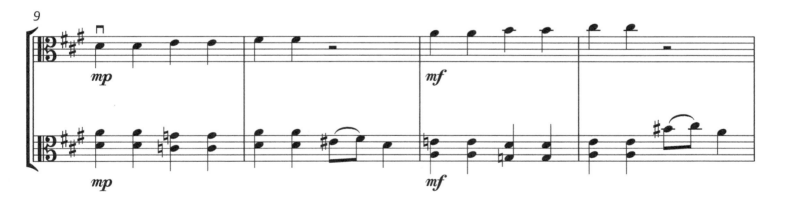

# 24. Daydream

C string special

KB & DB

**Gently**

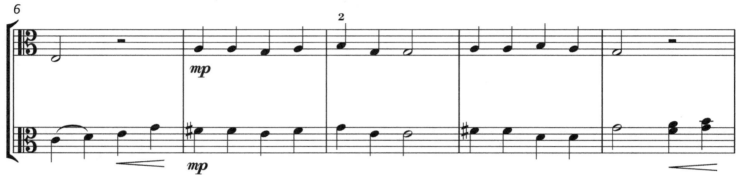

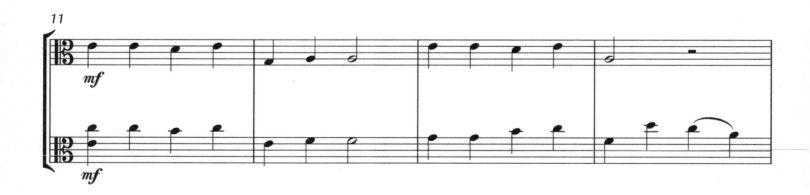

20

# 25. On the prowl

C string special

KB & DB

**With menace**

# 26. Summer sun

KB & DB

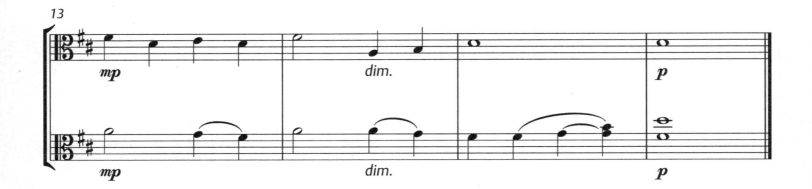

## 27. Phoebe in her petticoat

American folk tune

Swap parts when you do the repeat.

## 28. Ready, steady, go now!

KB & DB

## 29. Cooking in the kitchen

KB & DB

## 30. Happy go lucky (for Iain)

KB & DB

# 31. The mocking bird

American folk tune

**Gently like a lullaby**

# 32. Algy met a bear

KB & DB
Words anon.

Al - gy met a bear, a bear met Al - gy. The

bear was bul - gy, the bulge was Al - gy!

Swap parts when you do the repeat.

# 33. Listen to the rhythm

# 34. Cattle ranch blues

KB & DB

## 35. In the groove

KB & DB

## 36. Stamping dance

Czech folk tune

**Heavily**

## 37. Distant bells

KB & DB

**Slowly**

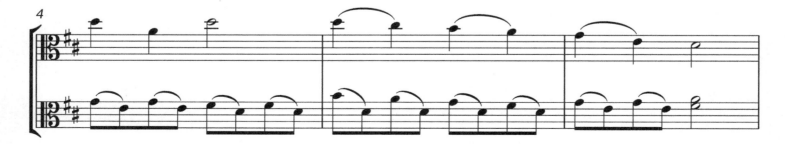

## 38. Lazy scale

KB & DB

# 39. Runaway train

KB & DB

**Express train tempo**

# 40. Rocking horse

KB & DB

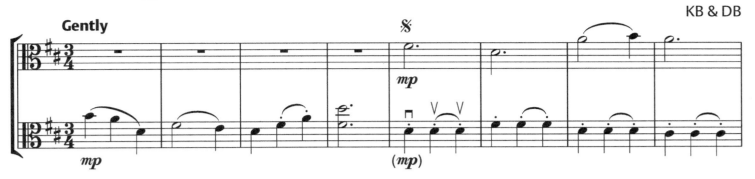

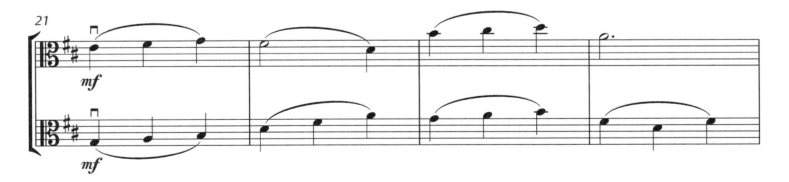

# 41. Patrick's reel

KB & DB

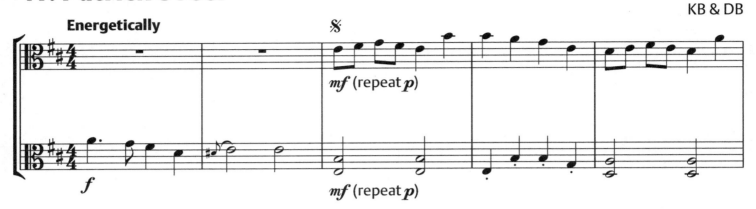

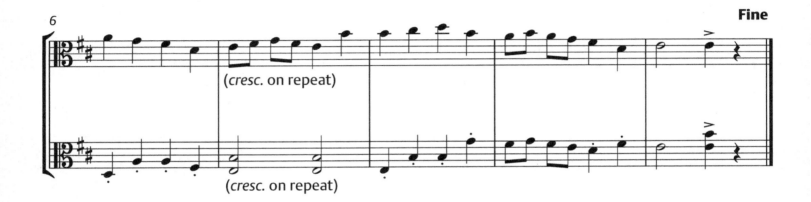

# 42. Calypso time

KB & DB

**Carnival tempo**

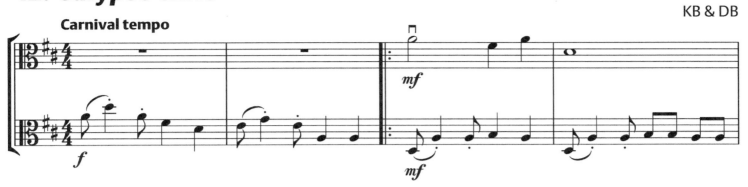

## 43. Tudor tune

KB & DB

**Lively**

## 44. Chopsticks for two

C string special

KB & DB

**Chunky**

# 45. Carrion crow

American folk tune

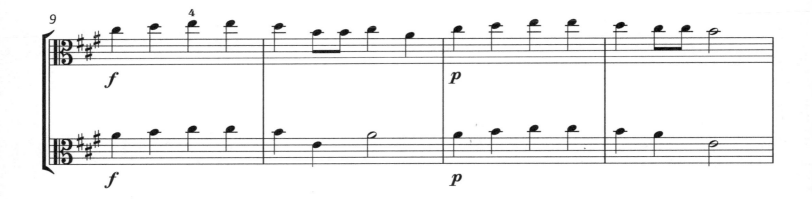

## 46. Flying high

KB & DB

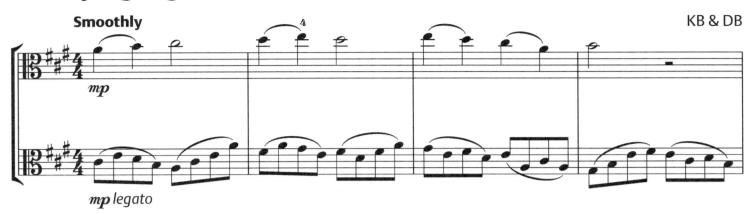

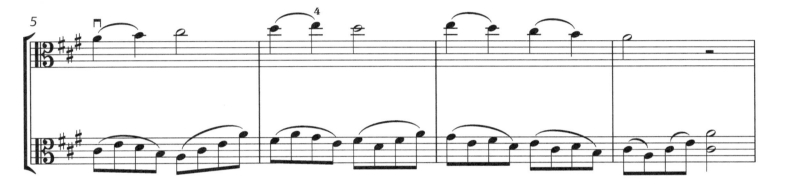

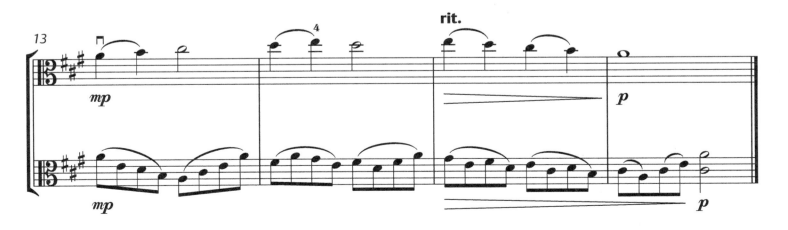

# 47. Viola Time

KB & DB

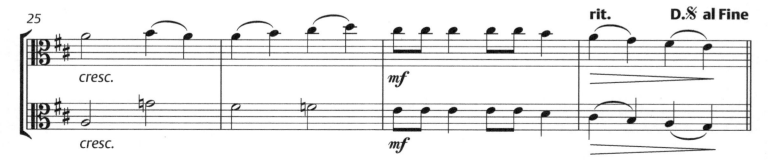